IT'S ONLY WORDS

Kristina Mahr

Copyright © 2018 Kristina Mahr

All rights reserved.

ISBN: 172038875X
ISBN-13: 978-1720388753

For the wonderers and the wanderers and you.

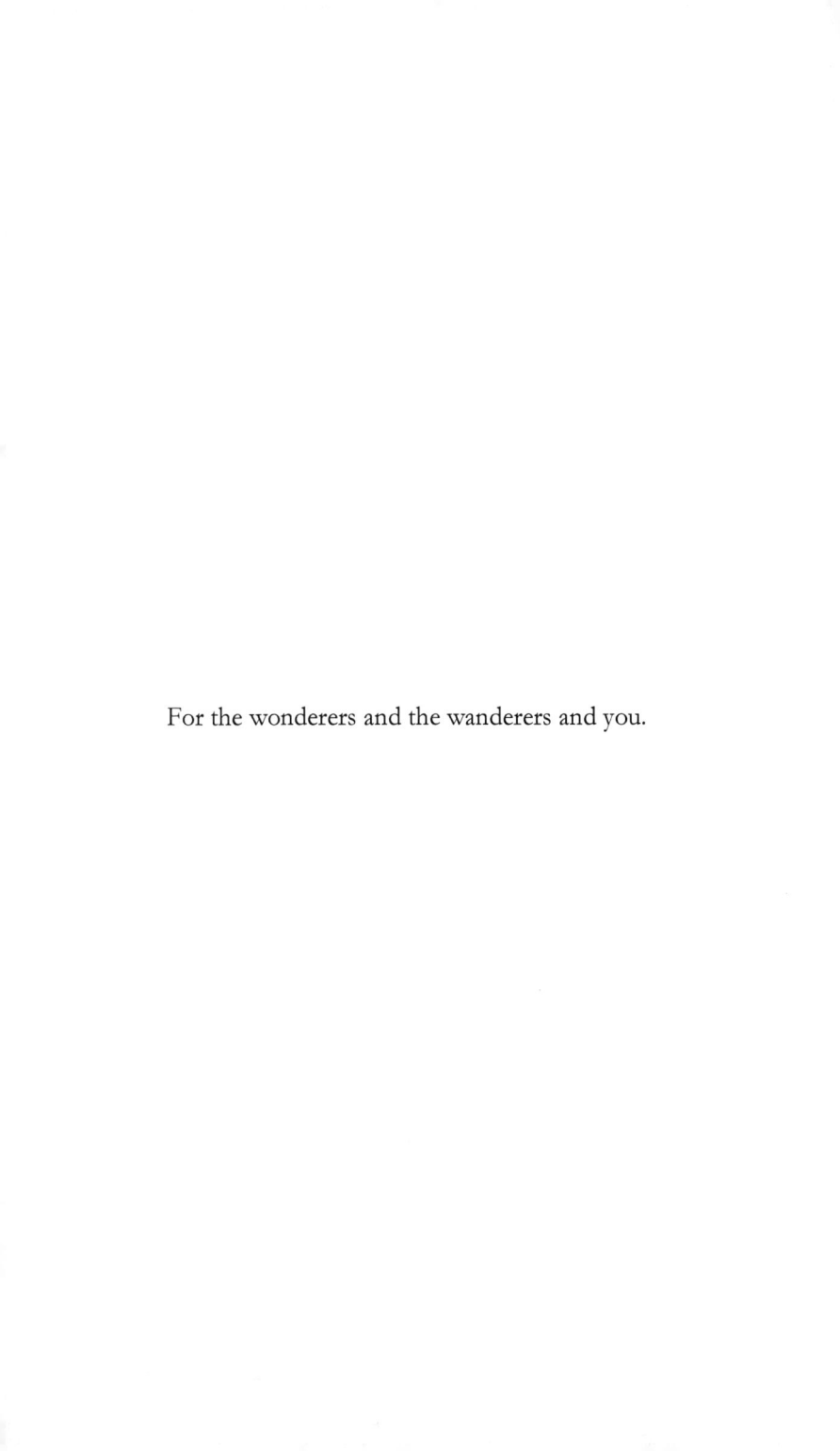

A NOTE

It felt wrong to arrange this in any way other than chronologically.

Here are the highs and lows, as they happened.
As they rose, as they plummeted.
Over
and over
again.

(I'm grateful for it all.)

(It brought me here.)

The Thing with Teeth

It was generous of Dickinson
to call hope the thing with feathers
and not the thing with daggers,
the thing with razors,
the thing with teeth.

Architect

I am an architect,
a builder of worlds.
I build worlds in your silences.

Half

I don't know how to stretch
back into a whole of me
once I've been a half of us.

Choose Differently

Sometimes I climb up into the attic
and put film into the projector
and watch it all play out.
I shout at the people on the screen
to choose differently.
To try harder, to say more.
To stay, to stay, to stay.

Beneath the Stars

I made a list of pros and cons,
and then I threw it out.
I went for a walk,
and I stood beneath the stars,
and I listened to my poor heart,
which had tried and tried and tried
but could not speak loudly enough
over my mind
until the stars gave it leave to bellow.

Because I Want To

Look, I've been walking on my own
for most of my life now.
I'm good at it.
I've got this.
So what I'm saying is,
I'm not holding your hand because I need to.
I'm holding it because I want to.

Broken Record

I am a record
that skips
and skips
and skips,
playing the same line in the song
over
and over
and over again.
You could fix it.
You could lift the needle.
But instead, you let it play,
and I keep playing that line,
the same line,
the line that says,
"I need more."

Circles

I talk in circles hoping
that you'll start doing the same,
and our circles will form a Venn diagram
with an overlap filled with words like
love, and yes, and this.

Love Is a Business Deal

I write my feelings on pieces of paper
and slide them upside down across the table to you.
Love is a business deal
with a price too high
to say out loud.

The Circus

You are a tightrope walker,
careful,
considering,
and I am an acrobat,
falling,
free.
You take each step slowly,
while I fling myself into the air and hope
(and hope, and hope)
that you'll abandon your rope
and catch me.

Kaleidoscope

We shift,
we blur,
we form something new.
I barely have time to soak it in before
we shift,
we blur,
we form something new.
Over and over,
I get glimpses and glimpses
of moments and moments.
We are a kaleidoscope
that I wish would stop turning.
I wish you would stay a little while.
But wherever we land,
at least I know –
it will be beautiful.

I Choose You

I know so little with any certainty,
but I know that happiness is a choice,
and you make me happy.
So every day that I choose you,
I choose happiness.
Every day that I choose happiness,
I choose you.

Letting Go

Letting go is as simple as
a hand opening
and as impossible as
breaking every finger of my own hand,
one by one,
in anticipation of also breaking my own heart.

I Turn Back

I turn,
and turn,
and turn,
until I start
to lose sight of you.
And then I stop.
I turn back.
For as much as my body
wants to turn,
as much as my mind
tells it to turn,
my heart won't let me
lose sight of you.

Come Back

I'm not asking you to stay.
My arms aren't a cage,
my hands aren't cuffs.
All I ask
is that when you're done
with what you must do,
when the world is too much,
when you're tired,
when you need a quiet place –
that I be that place.
That my arms be your pillow,
my hands be your balm.
I'm not asking you to stay.
I'm only asking that you come back.

The Best Answer

You are a catastrophe,
an upheaval,
utter chaos to my heart,
to my mind,
to everything
I thought I knew.
You are an exclamation point
unexpectedly appearing
in the middle of the sentence
that is my life,
and the best answer
to any question
I have ever asked.

I Pretend

I pretend that my heartbeats don't thud.
I pretend that I don't feel them,
that it's business as usual
inside of my chest.
I pretend that my smiles are more
than just gritted teeth.
I pretend that I mean them,
that they curve with something more like joy
and less like sadness.
I pretend that the world applauds,
that I take my bows,
that you
- *that you* -
are in the audience,
throwing flowers onto the stage
where I pretend that I am fine.

Except

For every two steps I take toward you,
you take one step back.
I should have caught up to you by now,
except –
except this isn't the way I want you.
Except I stopped.
Except I turned around
and retraced my steps
to where I did not love you yet.

Until It's Gone

Love rises in the east,
and it stays,
and it stays,
until the day comes
when it sets in the west.
When it falls down with the sun,
when it drowns in the sea.
Love stays until it's gone,
and I wish I could tell you
something more certain than that.

What It Doesn't Say

I am at war with the voice
inside my head.
The one that says,
"Nobody can drown you
if you don't let them
close enough
to hold your head under."
Because what it doesn't say
is that nobody can
save you then, either.

Finished

I wish you'd slammed the door.
I wish you'd yelled,
I wish you'd stomped,
I wish you'd done anything
but leave quietly,
but leave gently,
but leave so unobtrusively
that your leaving
felt like a lack of punctuation.
No period,
no exclamation point,
not even an ellipses.
Just an unfinished thought,
an unfinished sentence,
an unfinished us
that is somehow nonetheless
finished.

You Love Me Not

You pulled petals
from my body,
one by one,
leaving holes in my skin,
holes all the way down,
all the way through,
in my veins,
in my heart,
in my bones.
You love me,
you love me not.
You love me,
you love me not.
By the time you got to
the final one,
I didn't care which one it was.
I had already decided
you love me not.

Break Down

We didn't break up
so much as we broke down.
We ran out of power,
out of hope,
out of remembering
what it was
that we were fighting for.

Breakable

As tenuous as this felt
is as tenuous as it turned out to be.
There's a lesson in that.
There's a lesson in all of it,
but especially that.
Love shouldn't feel precarious.
It shouldn't feel as though
it's made of porcelain and masking tape
(while you stand over it with a hammer)
(while I stand next to it with glue.)
It shouldn't feel as though
it's balancing on a tightrope
draped across a canyon
(while you stand at one end with scissors)
(while I stand under it with outstretched arms.)
Maybe I don't know
exactly what love is,
but I know now
that this breakable thing
that you wanted to break
and I wanted to save –
this wasn't it.

For Me

Truth be told,
what makes this hard
is I wish I had not seen
how hard you fight
for everything you love
when you did not fight for me.

Later

I am a sea,
an ocean,
an entire goddamn universe
of unsaid words.
I saved them all for later.
(I thought we had a later.)

Gone

I knew that you would leave.
I felt it coming like a freight train,
like an earthquake,
like the ground was shuddering
beneath my feet.
I should have prepared more, I suppose.
I should have bolted down my bones,
stored away some blood,
put cushions around my heart.
Instead, I let myself feel it all.
Every jolt, every roil.
I thought that way I'd believe it really happened.
I thought feeling would be believing.
Instead,
I am bruised and bloodied
and I still can't believe you're gone.

What I Deserve

"You deserve more"
is code for
"I don't want to try to be what you deserve."
It's code for
"I'm pretending this is for you
when really I'm just scared."
It's code for
"You deserve someone who stays,
and I'm about to be
the very opposite of that."

That Scene

I've stopped playing that scene through in my mind.
The one where you come back.
Now I play the one where you stay gone
and I move forward
and I'm happier than I was ever going to be
in the one where you come back.

I Paint You

I paint you in my memory
as I wanted you to be.
I pull little moments that were real –
the magic ones,
the haunting ones,
the ones I cannot shake –
and I stretch them until they cover everything,
everything,
everything.
I do us a disservice,
but I don't have the colors,
I don't have the will,
to paint us as we were.

September

September was for you,
and I think it always will be.
Autumn, winter, spring.
I don't know you in the summer.
I don't know the shape of you,
the rise and fall of you,
the taste,
the smell,
the sound of you
in the summer.
You can't haunt me in the sunshine,
in the heat.
I think I'll go mad for missing you
the whole rest of the year,
but the summer is for me.

Ferry

Sometimes when I close my eyes,
we're still sitting there,
on that ferry,
and I'm still shivering beneath your coat,
and you're still pointing out the stars,
but this time when the boat docks,
we don't get off.
We listen to the dolphins chatter,
and we watch the waves dance,
and we are safe
from everything that came next.

Demons

Your demons have never
played well with mine.
Yours push
(me away,)
mine pull
(you closer.)
Yours fight for air
while mine gladly drown.
Yours are already looking
ahead, ahead, ahead,
while mine can't stop looking
at you.

Missing

How quickly you went
from everything to nothing.
From here to gone,
from bellowing to silence.
I miss the noise of you,
the fact of you,
the all of you.
I miss,
I have missed,
I am missing.

Love Is

Love is a memory
that fades unless you want it to.
A well that someone seals
with you still at the bottom,
screaming.
The roots of an ancient oak,
breaking through brick
and tripping those who try to run.
A hand that forgets what it's holding
and so lets go.
Layers upon layers upon layers
of paint,
too easily scratched.
Love is done and undone,
doing and undoing,
here
and then
gone.

Hellfire and Heartbreak

I am in the mood
to set fire to the sky.
To lie on my back
on the green, green grass
and point out clouds shaped like
hellfire and heartbreak.

Sidewalks and Chalk

I am sidewalk-carved,
cracking and caving and permanent,
too full of gaps
wherein weeds can grow.
You lay beside me there
and held my hand,
but you were not,
and perhaps are never meant to be,
carved like me.
Instead you drew yourself in chalk,
hastily scribbled,
too many colors,
vague and growing more so every day.
Gone, gone, gone
when the first rain came.

Imaginary Things

Starting over is waking up
in a room you don't recognize
from a nightmare
that doesn't stay in your sleep,
hoping that one day
you'll have your old room back
and your nightmares
can go back to being filled with
imaginary things.

As Though

They told me to follow my heart,
but I kept ending up on your doorstep.
"Stop," they said.
"Follow it somewhere else."
As though there are pieces
in other places.
As though I rationed it.
As though all of it
isn't yours.
As though I planned ahead for a time
when all of it was yours
but I was not.

Caution

I'm taking down the yellow tape.
My heart is no longer a crime scene.
I don't need to leave the pieces
where they lie anymore,
studying them
and trying to figure out
what went wrong.
I don't need to find
someone to blame.
It was just in the wrong place
at the wrong time.
(Some nights I wake up afraid
that it was only the time
that was wrong.)

Fireflies

We were fireflies in a jar,
captured in cupped hands
on a lovely summer night,
holes poked in the lid,
but glowing a little less each day.
We were beautiful,
we were bright,
but we weren't meant to last.
Not like this.

Gravity

This broken heart is gravity
turned up a little higher.
Pressing, pressing down.
Remembering
but forgetting a little more each day
how it felt to float, to fly.

On My Own

You pushed me into this pit
and did not stop to see
if I could find my way out.
I built stairs out of things
that had no business being stairs.
Ugly things and sharp things,
things shaped like nightmares
and things shaped like rage.
But they got me out.
You do not get to know
about any of them.
All you need to know
is that I did it on my own.

I Think I Used To

I think I used to love you,
though the reasons are fading
under the weight of your absence.
Under the weight of your apologies
where they fall flat against my ears,
across my back,
crushing and crippling and cruel,
twenty, thirty, forty lashes
for a crime I did not commit.
How dare you tell me
that you were doing this for me.

Ways That Stay

I scratched my love for you
into my skin,
under my clothes,
ugly and unruly.
I carved it way down deep
in a way that was always
going to leave scars.
I thought that they would haunt me now,
these scribbled words
that I will never not have on me,
and you long gone,
long gone,
but I wear them proudly.
I wear them as proof
that I do not love in ways that fade.
I love in ways that scar.
I love in ways that stay.

Does It?

I woke to sunshine
dancing across my closed eyelids,
and for a second,
it was flooding in
through a different window,
in a different life.
I let myself stay there,
in that life,
for a dangerous moment
before sleep wholly fell away
and my toes stretched out to touch
nothing but sheets,
just empty sheets.
I'm wearing the dress I wore
on our first date.
Does any of this
mean anything to you?

Rabbit's Hole

I followed you down
a rabbit's hole
where down was up
and sweet was sour.
Where I forgot things I once knew
and learned things that were not true.
I followed you down,
and you left me there
to find my own way back.
I cannot for the life of me remember
why I ever let go of your hand.

The Kind I Cannot Win

I stay up late sometimes
and play a game,
the kind I should not play.
I think of things you said
and try to decipher
truths from lies.
Some nights I make them all lies
and fall asleep hating you.
Other times I make them all truths
and fall asleep missing you.
It's the kind of game
I should not play
because it's the kind I cannot win.

Boy of a Man

What a boy of a man you are,
with your half-formed wings
and your reckless smile.
With your penchant for running
and never looking back,
never looking back.
With your sunshine laugh
and your moonlit apologies,
pouring whiskey down your throat
like life can't touch you,
like love can't touch you,
like I can't touch you.
What a boy of a man you are,
not watching where you go,
not watching when I go,
howling at the moon
and spinning circles 'round the sun
like what you do
doesn't break hearts,
doesn't break souls,
doesn't break *my* heart,
doesn't break *my* soul.
Like we,
like this,
like you
aren't doomed.

Just a Little Bit

This hallway is full of open doors,
and I keep trying the locked one.
My fists are dripping blood,
and the hallway is filling with fire,
but I can't stop pounding at this door.
Save yourself,
says my brain,
for it is whole and sure.
Never stop knocking,
even if it hurts,
says my heart,
for it is still just a little bit broken.

This Is What I Remember

This is what I remember:
it was raining,
and you were driving,
and I could not look at you.
This is what I remember:
it was raining,
and I was crying,
and you asked me
to please say something.
This is what I remember,
this is what I remember,
this is what I remember:
it was raining,
and I hugged you goodbye
outside the airport,
and when I walked away,
I didn't look back.

Too Late

You tried,
you tried
to take it back,
but any time after it was said
was too late for it to be taken back.

Temporary

You were never meant
to be anything but temporary,
but I forgot that along the way.
I built permanent shelves for you
amidst my bones,
carved a permanent space for you
between my heartbeats.
I built a home for you here,
within myself,
and you let me think
that you would stay.
That just this once,
you would let yourself settle in
somewhere warm and pulsing
and lasting.
I am empty shelves
and gaping holes now.
I am reminded,
I am reminded,
I am reminded,
that to some,
forever is less of a promise
and more of a cage.

I Thank You

You left more kindly
than you ever stayed,
mostly because
you never came back.
I almost don't know
how to fall asleep upon
a pillow that's not wet,
but I'm learning,
and I thank you
for knowing that I did not know
how to be the one to go.

Every Step Back

I am two steps forward,
one step back,
except for the days
when I am no steps forward,
twenty steps back,
a hundred steps back,
every step back.
Back, back, back
to where my very bones
were held together
by the way you held my hand.

Wherever You Are

Night is slow to fall these days,
but oh how long it lingers.
I count stars differently
than I once counted sheep.
Desperately,
pleadingly.
On cloudy nights, I never can find sleep.
My bed is too big,
and there are too few heartbeats here.
Wherever you are,
whatever you're doing,
you will never
- *you will never* -
be able to say
I did not try.

I'm Not Here

I sing an eerie song these days,
its only lyrics
the things you said
the night you left.
There are holes in the sky
and holes in my eyes,
and all of them are dripping,
dripping,
dripping.
For a little while,
everything else spun
while we stood still,
and now I'm the one spinning.
Dizzy, stumbling, falling,
drowning in the drips
from the sky, from my eyes.
I walk through walls like they're not there.
I walk through life like I'm not here.

Everywhere

You,
with your startling laugh
and your tilted smile,
flattened onto pages,
into words,
becoming fiction,
becoming lore.
I will only ever find you there now,
and you –
you will find me everywhere.

Bittersweet

It was not everything
over the span of a life,
but it was everything
over the span of those months,
and it was something
over the span of my life.
It is not the end all, be all,
except for the times that it was.
It is past-tense verbs
and bittersweet now,
memories
and patchwork hearts.
It is,
and then it was.
It should've been,
and then it wasn't.
It always will,
even though it never will be again.

Your Name

Other people have your name, you know.
I have to say it sometimes,
and my tongue always trips over it.
It knows that that is a word
it's not supposed to say anymore
because it's a word that hurts,
a word that burns.
And when it's in the air,
when I hear it,
I feel for a second as though
I can't breathe,
as though it fought its way from my body
and tore holes in everything
it passed along the way.
But then other people keep talking
as though nothing happened,
as though it's just a word,
just a name,
and I am reminded that it is that now.
That it has to be that now,
when once it was
the only word
I thought I'd say forever.

I Forgot

How does a person
become a memory?
I don't remember,
I'm trying to remember.
Every star I wish upon
is dead already,
is missed already.
I shy away
when people who are not you
try to touch me,
and I don't think that will surprise you.
I am tinder
in a world of matches.
(I forgot, I forgot, I forgot.)

Tell the World

I dreamt that you called me last night,
after all this time.
Your voice in my dream
was just like your voice in my past,
just as deep
and just as sorry.
You've held me down in this ice bath
too long, too long,
and I've almost gotten used to
the feeling of no feeling.
I'm leaning,
I'm leaning,
I'm everything but falling.
Tell the world I'd hoped to see it with you.

Joyeux Anniversaire

I have one foot in the past today,
a home in a rearview mirror.
I see streetlights,
I see alleys,
I see reckless, reckless hope.
The clock struck midnight,
and I stayed where I was.
I stayed until the rising sun
stripped every bit of magic
from the night.
I can still see the way
your face fell
when I told you that I loved you,
and I am still waiting for my heart
to crawl back up
from where it fell down with it.
Someday,
someday,
it will be something else to someone.
- *Magic that stays through every sunrise.* -
My blood, my bones
are singing your name,
and just for today,
I will let them.

Tell Me, Please

Love is a rope I don't know how to cut,
or a steel cable that never can be cut,
and only time will tell me which.
I tug at it every now and then,
but it holds firm,
it holds steady,
it holds these truths to be self-evident
that love does not leave
as easily as it comes.
There are power lines down inside of me
that powered something vital,
though I don't yet know exactly what.
A light that lived behind my eyes,
a light in a tunnel that never ends.
Tell me, please,
where anybody goes from here.

Firefight

There was no room for me
in your firefight heart,
with its barbed wire borders
and No Trespassing signs.
Your heartbeat is a siren
I pressed my ear to many nights,
lulled to sleep by
chaos and catastrophe.
Can you still see the patterns
I traced across your chest
before my fingertips turned bloody
from holding on too tightly?
I press down on my own chest now
on nights that are too quiet
and will my stuttering heart to remember
how to beat without you in it.

Almost as Much

Autumn is a Grim Reaper
I greet with open arms.
Show me, show me,
how beautiful dead things can be.
I think I will blend in more
when the branches are all left bare.
Inhale every bit of the universe,
and exhale the parts that hurt.
Remember, remember,
the things that are worth fighting for
(and all of the things that aren't.)
I miss when you were mine
almost as much as
I miss when I was yours.

Cured

Don't worry, don't worry,
my heart isn't bleeding anymore.
Here, take your gauze back,
it's cured.
Come sign your name at the bottom
of this new hard shell casing;
I want to give credit
where credit is due.
I am keeping the No lit
on my vacancy sign
for just a little bit longer.
There is barely even room
for me in here these days.

Drowning

I got so used to drowning.
All this pain
in the months since you left
is just my lungs remembering
how to breathe in air.

A Bouquet of Words

Did I imagine everything?
I could have sworn there were moments
I wasn't alone.
No matter where I am,
no matter where I go,
there is a part of me
clawing its way back to you.
(I contain it.)
Here, I picked you
a bouquet of words.
Please tell me that they're beautiful;
please tell me that I'm beautiful.
- *I don't care, I don't care.* –
I am anchored by memories,
for better or for worse,
and lately,
it's only for worse.

Tell Me a Story

Tell me a story.
(It doesn't have to be true.)
A butterfly flapped its wings
an ocean away,
some place beautiful,
some place free,
and you woke up that morning
with feet primed for running.
"All children, except one, grow up."
Wendy, darling, tell me a story.
Tell me how you knew
it was time to go.
Tell me how
you walked away.
Tell me how
you didn't
run.

Layers

I still believe in you,
like a child believes in Santa
even after seeing her parents
putting presents under the tree,
which is to say,
foolishly.
Sometimes I trace the lines of my hands
and wonder what they've held,
and wonder what they'll hold.
- *Multitudes.* -
And then sometimes,
I think of the lines of your hands
and how you washed those hands
so clean of me,
you must have taken a layer of skin with it.
The layer I touched,
the layer that used to touch me.
As for me, I have kept all of my layers,
unwilling to part with these scars –
they're the only gift
you ever gave me.

Already Gone

There is tape hanging from your ceiling,
and your fan is two speeds too high.
If you shook me, I would rattle,
full of words I cannot fathom into sentences.
But instead, you hold me,
and I miss you,
even though you're there.
But instead, you hold me,
and I miss you,
because I know
you're already gone.

Penelope

A lesson, my dear –
burn the bridge,
save yourself.
- *I know everything I need to know now.* -
I want to tie a rope around
every time I told you I loved you
and pull it back to me,
cover it in bubble wrap,
store it away.
I want to mold it into
something beautiful,
something true.
I'm weaving this shroud every day
for everyone to see,
and every night when I'm alone,
I undo the work I've done.
I will move on when it's finished,
I tell them, I promise.
I will move on when it's finished.

All I Take Back

A hundred thousand songs
about broken hearts,
and I still don't understand
how anyone survives it.
- *How does anyone survive it?* -
Forget me, forget me,
you said,
as you carved your name into my bones.
I take all of it back,
I take none of it back,
all I take back is
every time I ever apologized
for wanting more from you than silence.

Every Night

I'm not the praying kind,
but every night,
I ask the stars to keep you safe.
Can you see them where you are?
Do they tell you about me?
Do they tell you
that my dreams are coming true,
but that when my mind wanders,
it's still always straight to you?

Bent

I thought that we were bent,
you decided we were broken.
You decided, you decided,
everything turned on you deciding.
You decided I wasn't worth
whatever this was going to take.
Life is made up of choices,
and I have learned to be grateful
for everyone who chooses to stay,
even when it's hard
(especially when it's hard.)
"Do you still miss him?"
they ask me,
and I am teaching myself
to lie.

What I Wanted

I never wanted you
to be
anyone other than
who you are.
I just wanted
the you who you are
to want
the me who I am.

Not Anymore

There's a voicemail on my phone
that I don't listen to anymore
because it's hard to hear your voice.
(I keep it just in case.)
Trust was a bridge
we built of styrofoam and silence.
How did we ever think it could bear our weight?
There's a corner of my couch I don't sit on,
a show I don't watch,
a song I don't listen to.
A wish I don't wish,
a hope I don't hold.
A life I don't lead,
a person I'm not.
A person I was,
I think, I thought,
but a person I'm not anymore.

Let Me Show You

Tell me about the morning you woke up
and decided you didn't want to hear the ends
to any of my stories.
- I have never stopped wanting to hear the ends to yours. -
I am filling my hands
with other things now.
Keeping them busy,
keeping them here.
This is the way you left me.
Stop closing your eyes,
let me show you –
these unfinished stories,
these empty hands.
This is the way you left me.
Stop closing your eyes,
let me show you.

Folded

I am finely creased and tightly folded,
crumpled and uncrumpled,
crumpled and uncrumpled.
I am not scratch paper
for errant thoughts
and half-formed feelings.
I am not meant
for boys who only write in pencil,
who erase and are erased.
I want someone
who presses so hard,
it bleeds clean through.
Unfold me gently,
unfold me slowly,
unfold me like I'm a forest
and you're a match.
Carefully, carefully,
but like you want
to watch
me burn.

In Pieces

See how I bare my teeth
at strangers who call me pretty.
(*He knew me better and did not think so.*)
See how each step is a stumble,
how I skin my knees and elbows,
how I ignore the dripping blood.
(*Follow it, follow it, it will lead you straight to me.*)
See how my laugh is without humor
and my words are without polish.
(*Jagged and uneven, ripped to shreds before I speak them.*)
See, come closer,
come closer and see –
I am half-feral
with my heart in pieces.

Then Why

I read stories that remind me
of what love is supposed to look like.
- *It isn't this.* -
Thunder is a whisper now,
drowned out by all of the things
I didn't say.
(Why do we always think we have time?)
The only promise you ever made me
is that you wouldn't disappear.
But if you're still somewhere,
but if you're still anywhere,
I can't find you.
But if you're not somewhere,
but if you're not anywhere,
then why are you still
everywhere?

Scatter Me

So many romantic lines
about rising from the ashes,
about rebuilding from the ruins,
but I am learning,
but I have learned,
that nothing grows on scorched earth.
- *I am scorched, I am ash.* -
I post No Trespassing signs
for those who think
to plant gardens here.
- *Look elsewhere, look elsewhere.* -
(I am scorched.)
(I am ash.)
Scatter me to the wind.
I'll do no one any good here.

When They Go

This hope-tinted fear
the color of broken,
the shape of wanting.
I am reaching
and yet afraid
that someone will grab hold of my hand.
Look at the horizon,
so far away and steady.
Don't look down,
at the waves crashing against my feet.
- I am haunted by the rise and fall of it all. -
(By going, by staying.)
I still want the things
that I have always wanted,
but now I know
they forget to leave footprints
when they go.

Bury It Alive

Go ahead.
Bury it alive.
Dip your toes in freedom.
You let go
and I held on
and we will never
(*and we will never*)
agree upon
which of us was stronger.
Keep shoveling dirt
on your own beating heart
until it's all that's in your veins.
Someday, someday,
this will all be yours to regret.

How

How imperfect we were,
how razor-burned
and tear-stained.
How broken-wished
and phone call-missed,
how forgotten,
how misremembered.
How far gone,
how lost, unfounded,
how dreamt,
how felt,
how wanted.
How none of it,
not one of it,
not one heartbroken drop of it,
matters
in the face of
how I loved you.

You Cannot

The beauty of being left with no answers
is that I get to pick my own.
Like wildflowers, like daffodils,
like weeds when the mood strikes me.
(*A vase on every surface, a bouquet in every vase.*)
There is a hole in the sky
in the shape of you,
and look at all of the light shining through.
My hair is still saltwater damp,
is still wind-blown,
is ever in the way.
I carry the outline of your hand
inside the palm of mine.
(*You cannot take it from me.*)

For You

I have things to say.
Do you hear me?
I am made of stories,
raveling and unraveling,
colliding and collapsing
and in need of being heard.
- Everything I say is a bellow. -
I am the kind of art you can't hang in museums.
I am graffiti,
I am all-night noise,
there are song lyrics whispering across my skin.
Do you hear me?
I wrote this one for you.

Morse Code

Do you know Morse code?
I think my heart is beating it inside of me.
It's tired of relying on my mouth to speak.
Listen to it, listen to it,
skipping and stuttering its way through
I love you.
(How sweet it is, how precious.)
Crack open my ribs
and pull it out,
it's yours.
It does not speak for me.

Ships in the Night

We were only ever meant to be
ships in the night,
only meant to cross paths
and continue on our way,
but we threw ropes across
from your deck to mine
and my deck to yours,
and we held on for dear life.
Until the storms blew through and frayed them,
until the sun came up and blinded us,
until you started looking off toward the horizon.
You dropped the ropes and sailed away,
and I looked down at the blisters on my hands
and suddenly remembered
there was somewhere else I was supposed to be.

Bookmark

I put a bookmark where we stopped
so that we wouldn't lose our place.
I carry the book with me.
I still dream you under October skies,
under reds and golds and biting cold.
You are still quicksand for my mind.
I can't unthink you
once I've thought you,
and I think you all the time.
Look at my lungs, so full of sand.
- *I breathe around it.* -
I put a bookmark where we stopped
because we never reached the end.
I'll save our place for us.

Send Me a Picture

Send me a picture
of where you've gone.
A polaroid of what freedom looks like.
Cover the back of it with words that sound just like
I'm sorry.
Put it in an envelope
with a list of stories
you almost called to tell me.
I hope that you're remembering to breathe.
Climb out of where you've fallen,
if you can,
and send me a picture
of who you are without me.

Until I'm Ready

I just want to rest for a moment
and fold up inside of you
and let the world forget me
until I'm ready to be remembered.

My Happy Place

My happy place is a couch
beside a Christmas tree,
long after the season's passed.
I read you all of the words on my skin,
and you compare the sizes of our hands.
I want to tell you then
that though mine are small,
I know they can hold multitudes,
but the memory turns black and blue
when I'm reminded of the truth –
these hands could not even hold you.

Someday

Count to ten
and tell me again,
I'm sorry I'm slow to understand.
Hammer straight the curve
my stubborn spine learned
from nights spent pushed against you.
- *Fix me.* -
I tiptoe around fallen leaves these days,
I no longer find joy in their crunch.
(They had no say in the letting go.)
I know that someday
I will love somebody else.
That's all there is.
I love you, but
I know that someday
I will love
somebody
else.

Something Lasting

I'm sorry you dated a writer.
The blood can be dried,
just like it is,
and I will cut the wound back open
and root around inside of it
to pull out the memory of how it felt.
You can be gone,
just like you are,
and I will pull you back
to watch you leave me
again,
and again,
and all over again,
so I can turn it into words.
I can be fine,
just like I am,
and I will picture your face
and remember your voice in my ear
until my heart breaks all over again,
just so I can put it down in ink,
just so I can carve it into stone,
just so I can try to create something lasting
in a world where nothing ever lasts.

I Dance in Doomed

I dance in doomed,
oh, I rejoice in wrecked.
I frame letters I don't send
and invite strangers to read
the words you'll never see.
Grind your teeth
and drag your fingernails down
the paper skin of dreams you had
that could never contain me.
Paint your pastel rainbows,
swim in your sky of burning blues,
watch me, watch me,
how I spark and I shimmer
the same way fireflies do
before they
drop to the bottom
of glass jars never meant to hold them.

Desperate Bones

I blink and you're blurred,
I blink and you're gone.
- *I stop blinking.* -
Time pulls you from me
just like I wanted,
except now that you're going,
I grasp frantically at your edges.
- *Don't go, don't go.* -
The tips of my fingers,
the backs of my eyelids,
my ears and my hopes
and the tip of my tongue
are forgetting the shape of your name.
I wake up thinking about absolution.
I wake up
with desperate bones
bent into the shape
of who I was supposed to be.

An Inconvenient Flower

You wanted something pretty and stem-plucked,
something never meant to last,
and I came up with roots,
with ugly, curling roots
and a desire to be planted somewhere steady,
with inconvenient needs
like water,
like sunshine,
like air.
You should've left me where I was.
I had a chance out there.

Everything and Everyone

I am not fragile,
but some days I feel
a fault line running through me,
and I am scared of everything
and everyone
with the capacity to move me.

Reclaim It

I reclaim the shape of my heart
from hands that did not know how to hold it.
That crushed,
that dropped,
that forgot.
That didn't call,
that didn't write –
hands attached to bodies
claimed by boys
who looked like men
who ran
and didn't look back
and haven't looked back
and won't look back
and I –
I reclaim the shape of my heart
from anyone
who did not think it mattered.

Speak slowly around my edges,
tiptoe lightly through my thorns.
I've set this heart with splints –
it's been in need of realignment,
and you breaking it came
at just the right time.
- *It'll be stronger than ever once it heals.* -
I keep dreaming of you,
probably because I keep thinking of you,
most likely because I keep loving you.
Remember how hard it was
for me to learn to start?
You would not believe
how much harder it is
for me to learn to stop.

Paint Me a Sunrise

Raindrops trickle down
my reflection in the window,
I see a girl I know too well.
- *She isn't me anymore.* -
It takes a special talent
to hold on so tightly
to something that's already gone,
but then again,
did you see how well I held onto something
that was never even there?
Paint me a sunrise,
paint me a beginning.
Cover my walls
in as many colors as it takes
for me to remember who we were.

Innocence and Time

Listen, listen,
I was just wondering where I am.
(I hoped to know by now.)
Carve arrows into trees,
I've made a feast of all my bread crumbs.
My heart is a sieve,
my tongue is cement,
my veins are overflowing with wants.
- *Rattle me.* -
I can feel the brittle
crackle and curl
of the vines I no longer water –
the shriveled,
wretched,
reckless waste
of innocence and time.

The Better Question

When I close my eyes,
I'm walking backward,
and you are walking forward.
I'm rewinding,
I'm unspooling,
I'm only where I've already been.
When I close my eyes,
you're out of sight,
you were never even in it.
People still ask me
how you are,
and I think the better question
is who.

The Quiet Place I Go

We both know that you are not for me,
we know I'm not for you.
But you are still the silence
between each wild heartbeat,
the tangled and unyielding peace
I can't find on my own.
You cannot be,
but were, but are,
the only quiet place I know.
And so you are,
though you should not be,
still the quiet place I go.

I Want It All Back

The lights are off,
everyone else has gone home.
I've already lost it all,
I have nothing left to bet.
- I stay. -
I keep playing cards
that I don't have,
I go double or nothing,
again, again.
I can't walk away,
I don't know how to walk away.
(*I want it all back, I want it all back.*)

Aftermath

This heart does not know
how to break quietly,
it only ever roars.
It breaks in echoes,
reverberating off of my bones
in this well of a body.
(How many months deep is hurt?)
I keep my mouth closed now,
my lesson learned –
nobody wants to hear
the shift and shatter
bent and battered
aftermath of happiness.

These Words

These words are still about you,
but they're no longer for you.
They are pulled from my bones,
and you cannot have them.

Paper Airplanes

I'm tired of paper airplanes,
fold me something that will stay.
Fold me a ranch on a hundred acres
with a wraparound porch
and a pasture for our horse.
Fold me a joy-laced dog
with a penchant for running
and always coming back.
Fold me a song,
and I'll fold you a story,
I'll fold you a life,
I'll fold myself within you.
I'm tired of paper airplanes.
I'm exhausted by goodbyes.

A Fine Line

Leave me alone,
but don't go far.
There is a fine line between
loneliness and freedom,
and I dance from side to side of it.
I scribble thoughtless words
on scraps of paper
and set them on fire to stop myself
from sending them to you.
The first snowfall drips like magic from the sky,
and I can almost
- *I can almost* -
believe
that this won't be all there is for me.

The Only One, the Lonely One

In my head you miss me
and you wish things could be different.
Don't tell me if it isn't true.
I'm still blindly groping
the walls within me
for a switch I don't have.
An off switch,
a stop switch,
a pick up the pieces and run switch.
We both lost things
in this fire we set,
so why am I the only one trying to find them?
- The only one, the lonely one. -
If you're standing in the middle of the street,
screaming,
and nobody hears you,
are you really even here at all?

Never Better

I can't always breathe right anymore,
but I'm told I turn a lovely shade of blue.
And sometimes my blood spills out onto the floor,
and I wait for someone to comment on the mess,
but all they do is splash around inside of it
and thank me for making it so nice and cold.
My eyes look their prettiest,
oh how they shine,
with all of these tears within them.
And who needs to walk,
why bother standing,
when you have a perfectly good set
of hands and knees?
Oh I have never looked better,
I have never looked better,
everyone keeps telling me
that I have never
looked
better
than I do when I'm dead inside.

Smile

I am drip, drip, dripping
tears,
slip, slip, slipping
down
into
a pit
that once
was lit
but now it's
dark, dark, dark.
I am losing, losing, lost
now,
going, going, gone
now,
they think they've got
me figured out
now,
but I'm knee-deep,
but I'm neck-deep,
but I'm drowning, drowning, drowning,
and they're telling me
to smile.

Lullabies

I ran into the back of someone
while I was looking at the sky,
and he yelled at me to watch where I'm going.
- *Someone please tell me where I'm going.* -
I don't want to have learned anything from you,
but here I am,
with the color of your eyes
and the angle of your smile
as immovable facts in my brain,
but here I am,
with my arms held out
so no one gets too close.
You sing lullabies
through memories
on nights when I can't sleep.
- *They don't help.* -

Seashells

The waves whisper promises to the shore,
but then they leave,
but then they leave,
but then they leave.
We built sandcastles at low tide,
and everything was swept away by morning.
Don't you see?
You were born of the sand
and the salt
and the sea,
and I am just a girl
collecting seashells
to remind me that I was once here.

Frostbitten

I fell in love
through frostbitten fingers
that did not know when to let go.
I got used to chattering teeth
and the sight of my own breath.
Now I bury myself in blankets.
I bury myself in memories.
(Only one of those keeps me warm.)

The Hopeless Moon

The edge of the earth
is at the tip of my toes,
and I think I'm going to go.
- I am gutted by the hook of the moon. -
The hopeless moon
in the razor-edged sky
painted by hands
that shook and shattered.
The hopeless moon
caught on the rim of the breeze,
tucked in the dark of the night,
while the one that you're looking at
- shines. -

Wide Enough

I have a restless heart
twelve miles deep
and mere centimeters wide.
One step and I'm free,
one step and I'm scared.
- *Push me.* -
There is beauty in the streetlights
reflecting on the broken glass.
There is beauty in the blood
spilling slowly from my fingers
where I stoop to pick up the pieces.
- *Beauty in the hurting, beauty in the healing.* -
I want to fill frames with your face
and my bed with your body
and I want, I want
a heart wide enough
so you cannot have
left it.

Nothing Here

I have nothing here of you
but my own two hands that touched you,
but my own two eyes that saw you,
but my one lonely heart that loved you.
I have nothing here of you
but a raging in my ears
and a howling in my blood
and a rampant wish
that I cannot wish
for this to be
undone.

Hourglass

This hourglass ran out of sand
so long ago now,
and I cannot flip it over.
I joke that time stopped for me
the day you left,
and it's the kind of joke
where no one laughs
because I think I tell it wrong.
I spread my arms to walk the line
between my present and our past.
People ask me where I'm going
as though I'm not already gone.

Sharp Edges

Am I okay?
I am hollow in places
I was promised a heart,
I am inhaling razor blades
instead of air.
I keep tripping and falling over my regrets,
I keep picking thorns instead of roses.
I am shouting, I am wailing, I am pleading,
and no sound is coming out,
and he thinks that this is just how I smile
because he has never seen me truly happy.
He keeps trying to file my sharp edges
because I keep cutting him
when he pulls me too close,
and I push him away,
and I push him away,
because these sharp edges
are a gift from you,
and he cannot take them.

Snow Globe

Hold me up to the light –
I think I'm made of more than this.
I am a snow globe
filled with snow
that never settles.
(*I never settle.*)
- For less, for what everyone else wants for me. -
Nobody knows the things
that have been shaken loose inside of me
because nobody gets close enough
to hear the rattle.
I will never regret
any single thing I did
that I did in the name of love.

Closed

It is hard for me to love someone
who has eyes but chooses
to always keep them closed.

I Exist

Tell me again how sorry you are.
I need something empty
in which to store my hopes.
Stop pretending you want things you don't.
(Stop whispering my name in my dreams.)
I still remember the exact tilt of your head
when you said you didn't see another way.
As though things don't exist
if you refuse to see them.
As though things don't exist
if you
pretend
they don't.

Spotless

I am spotless,
I am straightened,
scrubbed
clean,
tidied,
there's no sign that anyone
besides me
ever lived here,
ever touched,
traced,
ever messed
up
my skin
my bones
the pulsing things
that lie beneath.
Go ahead,
dust me for fingerprints –
you won't even find
my own.
I don't live here
anymore.

From Their Own Fingertips

The tree branches keep reaching toward the sky
like if they stretch themselves high enough,
they can get back what they've lost.
I pat their trunks and tell them
to be patient, to be patient –
spring will come,
the sun will shine,
and what they miss
will grow back
from their own fingertips.

But Now

For a long time,
I went nowhere,
but now,
I walk.
I walk with splinters
in my feet, but
I walk.
For a long time,
I held nothing,
but now,
I hold on.
I hold on with slivers
in my hands, but
I hold on.
(To everything I have left.)
(To everything that's stayed.)
For a long time,
I missed you,
but now –
but now.

Flattened

It's hot in here,
and I'm draped in layers
of months since I heard
your voice.
How stifling, how suffocating,
how is it that
it gets heavier instead of lighter?
Each second an ounce,
each minute a pound,
each hour another crack
in my bones.
I am flattened,
I am floored
by all that could have
been.

Look at Me

It's been raining for three days now,
but I think that the sun would come out
if you would just look at me.
The earth is scorched,
but I think that the flowers would grow again
if you would just look at me.
My heart is broken,
but I think that it might heal,
I think that I might smile again,
I think that I might laugh again,
I think,
I think,
that I might *breathe* again
if you would just
look at me.

I Cannot

I press my ear to the wall,
and I discover
that silence has its own sound.
Like a rush, like a roar,
like everything
you ever said to me
and everything
you never said to me
echoing through my veins.
The end of the year is coming,
and I cannot
take you
with me.

What I'm Made Of

I never knew how many pieces
made me up
until I was in them,
and now
I can't stop rearranging them
and playing with them
and marveling over
all of their colors.
I won't thank you for much,
but I thank you
for showing me
exactly what I'm made of.

Wring Me Out

Oh wring me out
over the river
I thought
was shallow enough
to cross.
Watch the pieces of me
drown
in things
I'm never getting back
and words drip from
my throat as though
they've lived in there
for years.
Watch me try and try
and fail
to find
something here worth saving.

Hope

People ask me
what the hell
I'm still
holding onto,
and I tell them
hope.

What If

What if you
chase your dreams
and I
chase my dreams
and we promise
to look up
every now and then
to see if our dreams
have brought us
close enough
to one another
to reach out
and touch.

Green

You were a red light,
get out of the car and dance
though there's no music
sight,
a one-sided
unbridled
fistfight,
saying you will
when the truth was only that
you might,
starry-eyed
rambler
not meant for more
than that first
night,
the height
of broken,
the width
of sorry,
the depth,
the depth,
the goddamn depth
of gone
as soon as
the light
turned
green.

Go Ahead

Go ahead,
touch the stars –
just promise me
you'll come back
and tell me
how they felt.

Side to Side

I drew a line in the sand.
Things I can live with,
and things that I can't.
You move
from side
to side of it.
I drew a line in my heart.
Things I can't live without,
and things that I can.
You move
from side
to side of it.

Whens

I change ifs
into whens
and
I
wait.

Less Joy

Sometimes I lose sight
of where I wanted to go from here,
but then I realize
my eyes are closed.
Stop time,
rewind,
let me do it all again.
We may make more sense apart,
but oh,
we also make
less joy.

Pocket the Stars

I haven't slept
in three days because
you haunt me best
when I'm starved
for rest.
Eventually, though,
I'll have to sleep,
so I hope I'll at least
dream you.
The sky is falling,
falling,
falling
down
upon my head
and all I can think to do
is try
to pocket
the stars.

What If You Came Back

What if you came back
and
we straightened
the crooked parts
and
I didn't push but
you didn't pull
and
we didn't hide
from the rain
and
you didn't forget
me
and
we were the people
we used to be
instead of the people
we are now
with chisel fingertips
and hammer heartbeats
and your hand
over my mouth
and my scars
on your hands
and –
what if you came back.

In Shatters

I mostly miss you
in pinpricks these days,
except for the every now and thens
when I still miss you
in shatters.

Running out of Time

I am earth-pulled,
fallen-starred,
drowned in
better
days.
There is a sunset
in the curve
of your neck,
there are antelope
scattered
in the leap
of your pulse.
We fall too fast
and rise
too slowly
and I'm swayed
sideways,
I'm flayed
open,
I'm three shades too deep,
four stories too high,
knee-deep,
hands-tied
afraid –
that we're running
out
of time.

Unlikely

Someday I will stop writing about you,
but I do not think
it will be because
I've run out of things to say.

Save Me

I did not mind that you were sand;
I built a house on you all the same.
Look, our floor is made of
sand dollars and starfish,
fragile and alive.
I tiptoe around them
but you break more and more each day.
A message in a bottle
floated through last week,
with a note that just said,
"*Save me.*"
It floated through,
is what you said.
And I didn't ask
why it looked as though
you were about to
throw it out to sea.

Kites

You say that you love
flying kites,
but what you love
is watching the wind catch hold of them
and carry them as high as you have string,
and then letting go of the string
and walking away.

Nobody's Better

The past is bloodied,
dripping red,
its skin is buried
beneath
my fingernails.
My arms are months long,
my heart is never here.
Nobody's better,
nobody's ever been better,
at holding
on
to what's
long gone.

The Horizon

Go be the sea,
go flow,
go flee,
whenever the shore asks
too much of you.
I was that shore,
but now I'm the sky
and all I do is shine.
We both have better things to do,
we both bow before the pull of the moon,
but there will always be one place for us.
Kiss me,
kiss me,
at the edge of the earth.
Meet me
at the
horizon.

Wake Me Up

I fell asleep tracing
the scars on your back
and dreamt of firefights
and drowning,
of fireflies
and oceans.
Pull me down,
push me up
against the walls
you built
of brick
and fear
and
silence.
(Wake me up.)

February

I simmer in good
and burn in bad,
I still falter
under the throw
of the aftershocks.
It is too much
not enough
and not enough
too much;
it is a February
with too many hours
in too few days
and too many hopes
in too
few
hearts.

Shine

I am so many shifts and falls
that sometimes I forget
I can rise of my own volition –
I don't have to be pushed first.
So I rise with the sun
and again with the moon
and I never set
like I never settle
like I am draped in both
sunshine and starshine,
and aren't they the same,
isn't it all the same,
isn't this,
at last,
what the point
of you
has been.
(*To make me shine.*)

Watch the Sky

Couple of flight risks
fall in love.
(You know how this one ends.)
One saws off her wings
in a bloody mess
of feathers
and the fear of fear.
The other,
(you know this,)
he flies away.
And so all I do
is watch
the sky.

Just Look

Petals bloom
down the vine
of my spine,
but only
when
you touch me.
Look,
I want to say,
I'm not all
sharp edges
and storm clouds.
I can be soft,
I can rain
without
thunder.
Look,
I want to say.
Just look.

My Stars

I dragged my star
clear across the sky
to get it to where
yours was.
I can build constellations
out of whispered nights
and fingertip promises.
I can reroute orbits,
I can tighten
and loosen gravity
to hold
and to
release.
I can,
I can,
(I keep telling myself)
I can.
I can change my stars.
I just can't change yours.

Just Don't

I am strung together
by commas and em dashes,
by semicolons and parentheses.
(I don't know how to end.)
Pronounce me carefully,
whisper me out loud.
Make me a story,
make me a song.
Tell me,
sing me,
just don't
forget me.

I Guess I Keep Hoping

I guess I keep hoping
that if I scoop it all out of me
and mold it into words,
it won't live in me anymore.
This missing.
This breaking.

Sigh

I fell asleep
in the middle of a forest fire,
and my dreams burned
with the need
to save you.
You're slipping away.
(You're already gone.)
I inhale smoke
and exhale the way
you pulled me
against you,
into you,
all around you,
which is to say,
each exhale is
a sigh.
Which is to say,
I don't know how
to stop loving you.

Everything

You don't know
me at all
if you think
I'd walk away
from a door
just because it's closed.
Not when everything
I want
is on the other side.
Not until I've tried
everything.
And everything includes
waiting patiently
for you
to open it.

What I Really Want to Write About

I think that tonight I want to write about
the way that blue tastes,
the way that red feels.
The way I painted a picture that screams in its frame.
Does any of this make sense?
I'm so afraid that none of this makes sense.
That I carved senselessness from my senses
and became a window through which
it hurts to look.
I think that tonight I want to write about
the drip of ice cream down the side of the cone
and how I could never catch it all
with my tongue
and how I threw it away half-eaten
because I couldn't stand the way
it melted,
the way I couldn't stop it.
I think that tonight I want to write about
smiles shaped like forever
that forge words that taste just like goodbye.
Maybe,
after all,
after all,
what I really want to write about
is you.

Better Than Nothing

We weren't the best,
but we weren't the worst,
and that's something.
Something is always
better than nothing.
We were always
better than nothing.
(I don't think that's how I meant that.)
But we,
I know,
are better
than this.

Every Song

I keep drowning in too much,
and he spells *I'm sorry* wrong
when he writes it,
spells it like
you should have seen this coming,
spells it like
this is not my fault.
Stop digging around in my veins –
I've already given you all I could find.
Every song
is our song
because even the happy ones
have figured out
how to break
my heart.

What There Will Be

I don't want to be apart,
I want to be a part
of the stories you tell,
of the curve of your earth,
of the rise
and fall
of your chest.
I want to leave whispers
on your skin,
the shivering kind,
the kind
that could teach you
how to
stay.
I want to tiptoe
through
your dreams,
leaving echoes
in my wake,
and I want
there to be
tremors,
I want there to be
shatters,
I want there to be
you,
and I want there to be
me.
I want there to be
what there will be
instead of only
what there has been.

And I Need You

There are knots
in my necklace again,
and I need you.
(There are holes
in my lungs,
and I need you.)
I've been spun in circles,
but I'm only dizzy
when I walk away from you.
Somebody complimented the way
I can touch my toes,
and I did not tell them that
it was you
who taught me
how
to reach.

Too Much

It's never a question of enough –
I know what I am.
I know how I spill
and how I surge,
how I simmer
and how I roil.
I know how carefully I contain
the way I want,
the way I need,
the way
I say
your name,
like it's torn,
like it's shredded,
like I pulled it so hard
from my bones
that it came up in pieces.
It's never a question of enough,
but sometimes
I worry I'm
too much.

(Read Me.)

Run a finger down my spine,
and I will always think about opening.
Ask me what I contain,
which words will split me
into all of my pieces,
where I learned to write in blood,
why my heartbeats sound like sonnets –
and I won't even need to think about it.
(Read me.)

Show Him

I do not want to feel
this much.
The cool spring breeze
should not sting my skin,
water should not burn
as it slides down my throat.
I should not start to cry
because of a song
you used to sing me.
There are words
crawling up the back
of my throat –
I want to scream them.
(I swallow them instead.)
He holds me too tightly,
with my arms pressed
against my sides,
where I can't escape
the thud of his heart
and all I can think
is that
it's beating wrong,
he holds me wrong,
why
won't he
let go.
(Show him how you let go.)

But It Was

Today I came back to
a hole where
a home had been,
so I made a bed
of all the rubble.
There is gravel digging
into my spine,
ashes falling
in my eyes.
They tell me to move,
to build a home somewhere new,
like they're telling me
it's a quarter past two.
(Like it's obvious.)
(Like I'm a fool.)
Like a hole is not a home.
- And I'm whispering, "But it was." -

(How Could You?)

You haven't seen me
dancing around my kitchen
in my bare feet.
You haven't seen me free.
How could you,
when you were a cement block
tied to my feet
in the middle of the Pacific?
(How could you?)
Do you know my real laugh?
I don't know if I laughed my real laugh –
worry was always
so wrapped up in
my throat.
Sometimes I wonder
what stories you tell about me,
but I know,
they'll never really be about me.

Carefully, Carefully

I stretch moments,
I stretch memories.
Carefully,
carefully.
I cover the edges
of who we were.
(I hide the ugly parts.)
But it's been almost a year now,
and I can't stretch them that far,
that wide.
I can't cover the way
silence is a dagger
between my ribs,
the way you wield it
so well.
I can't stretch them that far,
and they're breaking.
They're tearing.
I throw the pieces of them
like confetti in the air,
and I let them hit me like pebbles,
like boulders.
(You would like the way they bruise.)

No Promises

I told you that
one of my biggest fears
is the ocean at night.
The way it seems endless,
but you know it must end.
The way your eyes
play tricks on you.
The way you see things
beneath the surface
that are not there.
I am less scared of the ocean now
than I am of you.
(The ocean makes no promises.)

(I Know I'm Tired.)

I think you're fading.
I think I'm gone.
I don't think
we were ever
here.
I think you're tired.
(I know I'm tired.)
I don't think
any of this
is what
either of us
wanted it
to be.

Who Am I Kidding?

I just want to exhale.
Do you understand
even a little?
I would take a little.
Who am I kidding?
I would take it all
and nothing less.
Who am I kidding?
I would take anything
you had to give.
Oh no,
not you, never you,
I was never kidding you.
I was carving answers from my chest
to questions you never asked,
dragging dull knives
across my rib cage
like the more it hurt,
the longer you would stay,
like the more it bled,
the more this must be love.
I think
(I know)
I was only ever kidding
myself.

Tangled

I am a tangle of a girl,
did you know that about me?
You can't pull
me free
of me.
Not even for a moment,
no,
not even for a heartbeat.
(Not even for you.)
I wrap limbs around
my limbs,
I pack
my organs
in ice.
I contain myself,
I contain myself.
And when I fall,
I make sure everyone
looks
away.
And when I fall,
I make sure nobody
hears
the crash.

A Little Bit Less

Some nights I hold my pen
so carefully,
so gently against the page,
afraid of what might spill.
These words, these words,
they were never meant
to hurt you.
I have only wanted them
to allow me
to hurt a little bit less.

I Guess You Didn't See It

I guess you didn't see it
in the curve of my smile.
"Don't leave me"
hammering against
my closed lips.
I guess
you didn't
see it.

For a Second, in a Dream

I dream a memory,
but I change it
halfway through.
I tell him suddenly
not to let go.
He looks confused and says
he won't.
But you will,
I tell him.
You do.
He shakes his head.
He promises,
he swears.
And through it all,
I know,
of course,
it's only a dream.
I know,
of course,
that he's
already gone.
But it's nice to see
the look on his face.
The way he truly thinks
he'll stay.
The way,
for a second,
in a dream,
it wasn't
just
me.

All I Ever Seem to Do

I've never been able
to keep my head above
love.
To float in it,
to swim in it.
All I ever seem to do
is drown in it.

All Along

I fell asleep.
(I'm sorry, I thought you knew.)
Everything you said
got washed away in a dream,
got swallowed whole in a nightmare,
got twisted,
got turned,
became
something
it's not.
You
became
something
you're not.
Or maybe,
or maybe –
you became what you'd been
all along.

All of the Love I Left You

What did you do
with all of the love
I left you?
Did you keep it?
I hope you kept it,
but in a drawer,
or in a closet.
I hope you didn't leave it out
where anyone could see it
and turn it over
in their hands.
I hope it meant
more to you than that.
And if you do
still have it somewhere,
I promise you
I will never take it back.
It will always be
the finest, purest gift
I ever gave
to anyone.

Holes

That sniper rifle boy,
how good he is at
hurting
from miles and miles
away.
I pull shards
from his exhales,
I plug holes
in the barrels of his guns
with my own fingers.
I try to save him.
I try to save myself.
I try to save us.
But in the end,
he pulls the trigger,
and the only thing I've managed to save
is a fistful of memories.
(Even those have holes.)

(I Needed You.)

I am a better person now
than I was with you,
but I'm also a better person now
than I was before you.
(I needed you.)
To break me so I
could rebuild me.
(*I needed you.*)

I Didn't Mean To

I've cried wolf so many times,
I'm not sure anybody's
listening anymore.
(Are you still listening?)
Somebody asked me
to draw a picture
of hope,
and I drew a hand
reaching out
through the darkness
for mine.
I drew an anchor,
I draw a buoy.
And I didn't mean to,
I didn't mean to,
but –
(I drew you.)

Only One

In the grand scheme of things,
you were only one raindrop
in the middle of a thunderstorm,
but you were the raindrop
that slipped through a crack
in the skylight on my bedroom ceiling
and landed on my cheek.
(You were the raindrop that woke me.)

Lost

I'm not naïve –
I hear the whispers.
(Even the ones that aren't there.)
I know I've passed
this point before,
but someone erased
all of the arrows I drew,
and now I don't know
which way to go.
I suppose I should stay
where I am
and wait to be found,
but have you met me?
You've met me.
I don't
know how
to wait.
(I'm too scared I won't be found.)

Remember

I had such a hard time
forgetting,
but that's nothing compared to
how hard
it's become
to remember.

Float

The current
keeps carrying
me back
to you.
I used
to struggle,
but now,
I lie
on my back
and float.

Safe Mode

If anyone asks,
I restarted in
Safe Mode
instead of
Normal Mode.
I was shut down
improperly.
Nothing was saved.
I don't know
how to do this
anymore.

Defy the Stars with Me

Some nights I wonder
who named all of the stars –
who pulled stories from their light
and from their dark
and from the fall and flash
of them.
If I could name any two,
I'd pick two at opposite ends
of the universe,
and I'd name one after me
and one after you,
and then I'd ask you
to defy the stars with me.

You've Already Forgotten

I don't want to alarm you,
but I stopped breathing
some time ago.
My body is curving,
caving,
collapsing
beneath the weight
of words
I never got the chance
to say –
they are
piling up
against my spine
and crushing my lungs
and setting fire
setting fire
to my bones,
and soon I'll be ash,
and all I keep thinking
is that if I am gone,
there will be nobody
to remember us.

A Choice

I don't know if you can call it a choice,
the way the sun rises,
the way the sun sets,
the way I am still
in love with you.
I don't know
if you can call it
a choice.

Fool

Call me a fool,
I don't mind.
I am always happiest
stretching my wings in places
where everyone warns me
the fall might kill me.
They're right,
sometimes it does.
But it's worth it
for the every now and thens
when I fly.

Things I'll Never Know

I still pick at the corners
of things I'll never know.
I am never going to stop
being who I am,
and who I am craves understanding
the way the stars crave a reprieve
from all of our broken wishes.
(It's so loud in here.)
My thoughts weigh
a thousand pounds,
and you don't help me
carry them anymore.
You can't.
Most of the weight
comes from
how badly,
how deeply,
how staggeringly
I wish
that you
were here.

Shadows

I don't know for sure,
it's just that there are
shadows pouring from the sky
and I can't find anywhere to hide.
There is love,
gasping for air
as I sob,
as I tell it over and over again
that I'm sorry,
that this is for the best,
that I can't find a way
to save it.
I don't know for sure,
but somewhere in this world,
I imagine someone else
is holding your hand,
and you are holding hers,
and she is so sure,
so sure,
and I want to tell her
that I was, too.

Anchor

I thought it was a good thing,
the way you anchored me.
You made sure I couldn't
drift away.
(I was so tired of drifting away.)
But then, you kept pulling,
and I kept sinking,
and it didn't matter
that I was drowning.
It never mattered.
You didn't let me up
until I was used to
water in my lungs,
and then,
you sent me back up
to rediscover air.
(It's not what I remembered.)

Unsalvageable

Untie me,
I'm in knots.
I have been
in knots over you.
Tangled, frayed,
unsalvageable.
I have been
unsalvageable
over you.

Lines

I am forever redrawing lines.
Erasing,
and trying again,
and trying again.
I redraw them
wherever I have to
so that you
fall
within them.

Raining Inside

I keep raining inside,
and everyone is looking at me,
waiting to see what I'll do.
I can't say your name anymore.
I can,
but I won't.
I shouldn't.
I don't.
I have learned that there's a difference
between wanting you
and wanting you
back.

Ransacked

I set you down somewhere,
and I cannot seem to find you.
I am ransacked,
within this skin.
You would not know it.
Doors flung wide,
drawers left open,
water rising,
water rising.
I am ransacked,
here,
now,
and everyone thinks
it was you
and how you left,
but it was me –
it was me
and how
you left me.

Doomed

You will hear in the silence
that I don't love you anymore,
but I wanted you to know
in this small place
just outside the silence
that the truth is,
loving you
has spread
to my bones,
and I am doomed,
doomed,
doomed.

CONTENTS

(How Could You?)	169
(I Know I'm Tired.)	172
(I Needed You.)	182
(Read Me.)	166
A Bouquet of Words	69
A Choice	191
A Fine Line	111
A Little Bit Less	175
Aftermath	108
All Along	179
All I Ever Seem to Do	178
All I Take Back	74
All of the Love I Left You	180
Almost as Much	66
Already Gone	72
An Inconvenient Flower	99
Anchor	195
And I Need You	164
Architect	2
As Though	39
Because I Want To	6
Beneath the Stars	5
Bent	76
Better Than Nothing	161
Bittersweet	59
Bookmark	91
Boy of a Man	49
Break Down	23
Breakable	24
Broken Record	7
Bury It Alive	85
But It Was	168
But Now	128
Carefully, Carefully	170

Caution	40
Choose Differently	4
Circles	8
Closed	124
Come Back	15
Cured	67
Defy the Stars with Me	189
Demons	33
Desperate Bones	98
Does It?	46
Doomed	200
Drowning	68
Every Night	75
Every Song	162
Every Step Back	55
Everything	159
Everything and Everyone	100
Everywhere	58
Except	18
February	151
Ferry	32
Finished	21
Firefight	65
Fireflies	41
Flattened	129
Float	187
Folded	80
Fool	192
For a Second, in a Dream	177
For Me	25
For You	88
From Their Own Fingertips	127
Frostbitten	117
Go Ahead	137

Gone	27
Gravity	42
Green	136
Half	3
Hellfire and Heartbreak	36
Holes	181
Hope	134
Hourglass	121
How	86
I Cannot	131
I Choose You	12
I Dance in Doomed	97
I Didn't Mean To	183
I Exist	125
I Forgot	61
I Guess I Keep Hoping	157
I Guess You Didn't See It	176
I Paint You	30
I Pretend	17
I Thank You	54
I Think I Used To	44
I Turn Back	14
I Want It All Back	107
I'm Not Here	57
Imaginary Things	38
In Pieces	81
In Shatters	143
Innocence and Time	104
Joyeux Anniversaire	63
Just a Little Bit	50
Just Don't	156
Just Look	154
Kaleidoscope	11
Kites	147

Later	26
Layers	71
Less Joy	140
Let Me Show You	79
Let's Start Over	102
Letting Go	13
Lines	197
Look at Me	130
Lost	185
Love Is	35
Love Is a Business Deal	9
Lullabies	115
Missing	34
Morse Code	89
My Happy Place	94
My Stars	155
Never Better	113
No Promises	171
Nobody's Better	148
Not Anymore	78
Nothing Here	120
On My Own	43
Only One	184
Paint Me a Sunrise	103
Paper Airplanes	110
Penelope	73
Pocket the Stars	141
Rabbit's Hole	47
Raining Inside	198
Ransacked	199
Reclaim It	101
Remember	186
Running out of Time	144
Safe Mode	188

Save Me	146
Scatter Me	83
Seashells	116
Send Me a Picture	92
September	31
Shadows	194
Sharp Edges	122
Shine	152
Ships in the Night	90
Show Him	167
Side to Side	138
Sidewalks and Chalk	37
Sigh	158
Smile	114
Snow Globe	123
Someday	95
Something Lasting	96
Spotless	126
Tangled	174
Tell Me a Story	70
Tell Me, Please	64
Tell the World	62
Temporary	53
That Scene	29
The Best Answer	16
The Better Question	105
The Circus	10
The Hopeless Moon	118
The Horizon	149
The Kind I Cannot Win	48
The Only One, the Lonely One	112
The Quiet Place I Go	106
The Thing with Teeth	1
Then Why	82

These Words	109
Things I'll Never Know	193
This Is What I Remember	51
Too Late	52
Too Much	165
Unlikely	145
Unsalvageable	196
Until I'm Ready	93
Until It's Gone	19
Wake Me Up	150
Watch the Sky	153
Ways That Stay	45
What I Deserve	28
What I Really Want to Write About	160
What I Wanted	77
What I'm Made Of	132
What If	135
What If You Came Back	142
What It Doesn't Say	20
What There Will Be	163
When They Go	84
Whens	139
Wherever You Are	56
Who Am I Kidding?	173
Wide Enough	119
Wring Me Out	133
You Cannot	87
You Love Me Not	22
You've Already Forgotten	190
Your Name	60

ACKNOWLEDGMENTS

For my family, who made me.
For my friends, who deepen me.
For the words, which free me.

(Cover design by Kingwood Creations.)

ABOUT THE AUTHOR

Kristina Mahr devotes her days to numbers and her nights to words. She works full-time as an accountant in the suburbs of Chicago, where she lives with her two dogs and two cats, but her true passion is writing. In her spare time, she enjoys spending time with her family and friends, reading, and waking up at the crack of dawn every weekend to watch the Premier League.

www.kristinamahr.com

Printed in Great Britain
by Amazon